DRUGS AND SPORTS

Drugs and sports do not make a good team.

THE DRUG ABUSE PREVENTION LIBRARY

DRUGS AND SPORTS

Rodney G. Peck

THE ROSEN PUBLISHING GROUP, INC.
NEW YORK

Published in 1992, 1997 by The Rosen Publishing Group, Inc.
29 East 21st Street, New York, NY 10010

Revised Edition 1997

Library of Congress Cataloging-in-Publication Data
Peck, Rodney G.
  Drugs and sports / Rodney G. Peck. — rev. ed.
  (The Drug Abuse Prevention Library)
  Includes bibliographical references and index.
  Summary: Discusses why athletes use different drugs, how they become addicted, the consequences of drug abuse, and how to get help.
    ISBN 0-8239-2565-X
    1. Doping in sports—Juvenile literature.
    2. Anabolic steroids—Health aspects—Juvenile literature. [1. Athletes—Drug use.   2. Drug abuse.]   I. Title.   II. Series.
  RC1230.P43   1992
  362.29′08′8976—dc20   92-12359
                                                           CIP
                                                           AC

Manufactured in the United States of America

Contents

Introduction

More than 6 million high school students in the United States play some form of organized sports. These include basketball, tennis, football, soccer, baseball, wrestling, and just about any other sport you can name. Many of these student-athletes have used or currently use some sort of drug during their athletic career. Some athletes use drugs to improve their performances. Others try drugs because their friends use them. Still others follow the example of drug use set by some professional athletes.

There are many reasons why people use drugs. In this book, you'll read about the most common reasons why athletes use drugs. You'll also read about the drugs they use most often and what these substances do to the human body. You'll find out how drug abuse actually hurts an athlete's performance rather than helps it. Finally, you'll learn how to make choices that are good for you both as a teenager and as an athlete.

Most young people enjoy competing in sports.

CHAPTER 1

Drugs and Your Body

You probably know that a drug is a substance that changes the way you think, feel, or behave. But you may not know how many substances are classified as drugs—the nicotine in tobacco, the caffeine in soda, alcohol, steroids, and medicine.

Drugs That Can Help You

"Good" drugs, or medicines, help your body heal when you are hurt or ill. It is okay to take medicine when a doctor prescribes it or when a parent gives it to you. It is not okay for your friends to take your medicine. What is helpful to one person may be harmful to someone else.

10 | *Drugs That Can Hurt You*

"Bad" drugs hurt your body. These include nicotine, caffeine, alcohol, marijuana, steroids, and a long list of others.

When someone uses "bad" drugs, it hurts his or her mind and body. It can change the way a person thinks about and treats himself or herself. It can also change the way he or she acts toward and treats other people. Even worse, a person can become addicted to drugs.

When a person is addicted to drugs, he or she craves the drug. The person believes that he or she needs the drug to feel normal.

How Does Addiction Start?

There is a pattern to drug addiction, and it looks like this:

Step 1. Casual use or experimentation
Step 2. Regular use
Step 3. Addiction or chemical dependence

Casual use of any drug is the first step toward drug addiction.

Shawn was a sophomore who landed a position on the varsity football team. He was excited about the first game. But he was also nervous. What if he dropped the ball? What if he fumbled a big play?

On the morning of the first game, Shawn
told a couple of the other players how he felt.
Josh, a senior, offered Shawn a marijuana
joint. He told Shawn to smoke it to feel more
relaxed—it would help him stop worrying
and focus on the game.

Shawn decided to try it. Anything was
better than looking like a fool on the field.
And it worked. He did feel more relaxed and
he played well that first game.

Shawn didn't realize that smoking the
marijuana actually slowed his body down.
He may have felt more relaxed, but his
body wasn't working as well as it could
have been.

Regular use begins when a person's
body builds up a tolerance to the drug.
That means that his or her body becomes
used to the drug. Someone who uses a
drug regularly needs more and more of the
drug to continue to feel its same effects.

Halfway through the season, Shawn was
smoking a joint before every game and some-
times before practice, too. Sometimes he
thought needed two joints just to relax.

Regular use moves to **addiction** when
a person continues to use the drug even
when it causes bad things to happen.

Cigarette smoking can lead to dependence on the drug nicotine.

By the end of his first season, Shawn was smoking pot every day. He felt as though he couldn't face homeroom until he smoked a joint. He began stealing money from his parents to pay for his stash.

His grades dropped, and his coach threatened to throw him off the team unless his behavior changed. The odd thing was that Shawn didn't care. All he cared about was whether he had enough pot to get him through the day.

Shawn had become addicted to marijuana. Addiction can happen with *any* drug. It can also happen to anyone.

Chemical dependence, or drug addiction, is a disease. A person who is chemically dependent on a drug has lost the ability to choose whether to use the drug or not. The person feels that he or she needs the drug to survive, even if using the drug hurts his or her body and life, and those people around him or her. The person feels as though he or she can't face life without using that drug.

Chemical dependence also includes alcohol addiction, or alcoholism.

Addiction Can Strike Anyone

Anyone can become addicted to drugs or alcohol. Addiction is not restricted to one group of people. It affects rich and poor, people of all races and religions, both men and women, athletes and nonathletes, adults and teens.

Teenagers can become addicted more quickly than adults. This is because a young, growing body builds tolerance faster than a mature body. Then the person taking the drug needs more of it to get the same high.

From Parent to Child

Experts believe that the disease of addiction can be passed down from parent to child. A teen who has a parent with an addiction (or a parent who is recovering from an addiction) may be more likely to become an addict as well.

Feeling the need to drink alcohol every day may be a sign of addiction.

However, not all children of addicts become addicts themselves. It just increases the possibility. If you have a parent who has or is recovering from an addiction, understand that his or her addiction directly affects you. You must be especially careful around drugs and alcohol.

Clues to Addiction

You know that drug or alcohol addiction is a disease. But do you know how to recognize addiction?

There are four symptoms of addiction. **15**
If a person shows two or more of these
symptoms, it is likely that the person is
addicted.

The symptoms are:

- Loss of control over the use of a
  drug;
- Continued use of the drug even
  though using it is causing problems
  in the person's life;
- A compulsion or need to use the
  drug again and again;
- Craving the drug when he or she
  doesn't have it.

Once a person has the disease of addiction, it never goes away. But with help, he
or she can get it under control.

Where Does Addiction Begin?

As we have seen, drug addiction starts
very innocently. It usually starts with
something called a gateway drug.

Tobacco, alcohol, and marijuana are all
gateway drugs. They are called gateway
drugs because they open the gate for
further drug use. People start with the
gateway drugs and end up using harder
ones.

16   When people drink alcohol or get high on pot for a while, they get bored and want to try something new. They think that they can use alcohol or marijuana without having problems. Then they think that drugs are not really as bad as people say they are.

Experimentation

Drug use normally starts during the teen years. Young people decide to "experiment" with gateway drugs for a lot of reasons:

- To forget their problems;
- To be cool;
- To seem older or more mature;
- To rebel against their parents;
- To do what their friends do;
- To be popular.

Using drugs does not make your problems go away. It only adds to the problems that already exist. Drugs do not make you cool either. Ask yourself, "What is cool about throwing up or passing out when you are buzzed?" Also, being mature has nothing to do with drugs. Being mature means that you make healthy decisions for your life. You should

Everything you put into your body affects you. Healthful foods are important for keeping your body in top condition.

do things because you want to do them, not because your friends want you to. The decision should be yours.

People who use drugs to rebel think that taking drugs will hurt their parents. That is true. Taking drugs probably *will* hurt their parents. It also hurts the

Loss of energy may be a symptom of a drug problem.

person who is taking the drugs. Taking drugs to rebel hurts everybody.

Peer pressure is a big problem to face. If you feel pressure to use gateway drugs, you will feel pressure to use other drugs, too. Don't give in to the pressure.

A healthy lifestyle that includes exercise, plenty of sleep, and a balanced diet is the best way to build a strong body.

CHAPTER 2

Anabolic Steroids

*M*any people believe that taking anabolic steroids, commonly known as steroids, will help make them stronger, faster, and better athletes. While it's true that steroids help build muscles, they also cause far more problems than they solve.

Steroid use is growing at a rapid rate. There are more than 3 million steroid users in the United States alone. The U.S. Department of Health and Human Services reports that 262,000 teens are using or have used steroids.

Sports requiring a lot of strength, such as football, wrestling, weight lifting, track and field, and swimming, have athletes who use steroids most often.

How Steroids Work

Our bodies make natural chemicals called hormones. Hormones control how we grow. The hormone in boys and men that controls muscle growth and height is called testosterone.

Steroids are chemicals, too. But they are made in a laboratory. Steroids, taken in pill or liquid form, are imitation testosterone. The liquid can be injected with a needle.

Taking steroids affects the way the body grows and functions. The human body is a perfect machine if it is treated well. It knows how much testosterone it needs to grow and develop properly. The extra testosterone from steroids confuses the body.

Taking steroids can cause a lot of problems for young men and women. People think that steroids will make them faster, bigger, and stronger. That may be true for a while, but it does not last. Steroid users have problems with their health. The drug also affects the way they think and how they act. More bad changes occur than good.

Steroids can also turn off the process that makes a teenager's bones grow. In addition, most young people who use

steroids get severe acne on their faces,
chests, backs, and arms. Some people get
bad headaches. Steroid users have high
temperatures more often than normal.
Some get nosebleeds; others lose their
hair.

The combination of steroids and the
human body can be deadly. Steroid
users develop a buildup of a fat called
cholesterol. This fat clogs arteries and
veins, making it harder for blood to get
through the body to the heart. The body
has to work extra hard to push the blood
through. Many steroid users end up with
damaged hearts. Retired NFL star Steve
Courson has a potentially fatal heart-
muscle disorder that he believes was
caused by his use of steroids for many
years. Some steroid users even have heart
attacks and die.

Steroids also turn off the body's hormone system, which causes other problems. The hormone system is part of the
reproductive system, which is responsible
for the sex glands. When your body's hormone system shuts down, so do your sex
glands. Some young men find that their
breasts get larger and their testicles shrink
when they use steroids. Young women
who use steroids may find that their

Drugs at a Glance

Alcohol: Alcohol can alter mood, cause changes in the body, and become habit-forming. Alcohol is a depressant. It slows the body down. It affects the central nervous system.

Signs of Use:
Bad judgment, loss of self-control and coordination, slow reactions, slurred speech, and sometimes blackouts.

Long-Term Effects:
Brain—Permanent cell damage, loss of memory, confusion.
Heart—High blood pressure, enlarged heart.
Liver—Swelling, cirrhosis.
Lungs—Swelling, chance of infection.
Sex Organs—Impotence.
Stomach—Ulcers.
Muscles—Weakness, loss of tissue.

Tobacco: Contains three dangerous chemicals: nicotine, tar, and carbon monoxide. Very addictive.

Signs of Use:
Shortness of breath, bad breath, coughing, asthma.

Long-Term Effects:
Heart—High blood pressure, possible heart attack.
Lungs—Possible cancer, pneumonia, emphysema, bronchitis.
Mouth—Possible cancer.

Marijuana: Contains over 400 chemicals. Causes mood changes. Addictive.

Signs of Use:
Memory loss, loss of coordination, loss of concentration, loss of motivation, unusual fears.

Long-Term Effects:
Eyes—Redness.
Brain—Brain damage.
Heart—Low oxygen supply.
Lungs—Possible cancer.
Sex Organs—Damages normal sexual growth.

Cocaine: Highly addictive. Changes brain chemistry.

Signs of Use:
Nosebleeds, loss of sleep, weight loss, depression, violent behavior, the "shakes," loss of interest, poor appearance.

Long-Term Effects:
Central Nervous System—Damage.
Brain—Permanent damage.
AIDS—Possible if cocaine is injected with an infected needle.
Heart—High rate, possible stroke or heart attack.

Crack: Powerful, smokable form of cocaine. Extremely addictive.

Steroids: Artificial male hormone. Dangerous to physical and mental growth.

Signs of Use:
Temporary increase in size, strength, and weight.

Long-Term Effects:
Brain—Drastic mood swings.
Heart—High blood pressure.
Kidney—Malfunction or failure.
Liver—Damage, possible tumor.
Skin—Tumors, acne.
Bone—Stops growth.
Sex Organs—Smaller testicles, infertility.

menstrual cycle goes off schedule or stops. They may become sterile, which means that they will not be able to have children.

Another health problem that can arise from steroid use is cancer. In many users, tumors develop in the liver, the kidneys, and the prostate. NFL football star Lyle Alzado died of brain cancer in 1992. He had used steroids for sixteen years. He was addicted to them and continued to use them even after he retired from football. He believed that steroids caused his cancer.

Steroids also affect a user's mood and personality. Athletes who use steroids often have trouble dealing with the people around them. The increase in testosterone makes the athletes more violent. Things that wouldn't normally bother them may set off a "roid rage." ("Roid" is a nickname for steroid.) A user loses control of his anger and takes it out on everyone around him or her.

People who use steroids often lose their memories. They can't concentrate for very long. They also lose their ability to cope with stress.

In addition, steroids can cause athletes to lose their ability to feel pain. For

26 | example, if a swimmer pulls a muscle in her shoulder, she may take a steroid injection so she won't feel the pain while swimming in an upcoming meet. If she damages the muscle more, she still won't feel it. She could destroy her swimming career by using the steroids and severely tearing a muscle.

The High Cost of Steroids

The physical and mental costs are not the only price that steroid users pay. Steroids also cost money. Steroids are prescribed by some doctors for specific problems. But most steroids are purchased illegally.

The price of illegal steroids depends on the dose. The average steroid user spends between $50 and $600 per month. The illegal sale of products is called the "black market." Today, the black market supplies 60 to 80 percent of the steroids used. Steroid pushers are making between $300 and $400 million each year.

CHAPTER 3

Why Athletes Start Using Drugs

Some people start using drugs in middle school. Others start in high school. Why?

Peer Pressure

The most common reason that people use drugs is peer pressure. They start using drugs when their friends or team-mates offer them some. Nobody wants to be called a "wimp" or a "goody-goody." Many people eventually give in to the pressure. They think that if they don't use the drug, the rest of the team won't like them.

This is negative peer pressure—when you feel pressure to do something that you don't want to do. Negative peer pressure

The problems of a drug user will affect every family member.

is tough to face, especially if you're facing a lot of people at once.

However, peer pressure does not have to be negative. Peer pressure can also be positive. Does your team have rules about drinking? Or about smoking or using other drugs? Those rules can be used for positive peer pressure. You can remind your teammates of the rules. You are not the only one who thinks that rules are a good idea. If your team does not have rules about drug use, maybe you could suggest having them. The rules need to state clearly the penalties for drug use. Talk to your coach or trainer.

There are other ways to use positive peer pressure. For example, don't go to parties where there will be alcohol or marijuana. Instead, throw a party of your own. Have rules about guests coming sober, not drunk or stoned. That is a great way to boost positive peer pressure. It shows people that they do not need alcohol or other drugs to have fun.

If someone on your team is using drugs, try to encourage him or her not to use them. Be a positive role model. Try to get other team members to talk to the person. Show your teammate that the

Teens can be popular with friends by being drug-free and having a positive attitude.

team cares. Positive peer pressure is more powerful than negative peer pressure.

To Be "Cool"

Some people start using drugs to be "cool." They drink alcohol to look older and more mature. They smoke pot or snort cocaine because it is the hip thing to do. If the popular people are doing it, others usually follow. They wrongly think that using drugs will help them be accepted by the popular group.

People become popular for many reasons. Some are popular because they are smart. Some are popular because they are talented in music or drama. Others are popular because they are student leaders.

Many people are popular because they play sports. Being an athlete carries a lot of responsibility. Athletes represent their school—other students and teachers—and the whole town. It is important that they set a good example. They serve as role models for their peers and for younger people.

A responsible athlete is someone who thinks that being drug-free is cool. The only way to be popular and cool at the same time is to stay away from alcohol and other drugs.

To Look Good

Peer pressure to look good is another reason that athletes start using drugs.

Girls in our society are expected to be thin. They are expected to have perfect breasts, flat stomachs, and slim hips. It's silly, but some people think that is how the ideal girl is supposed to look.

Parties can be fun without alcohol and drugs.

More and more young women are
turning to drugs to try to achieve "the
look." Thousands of women use diet
pills to lose weight. Other young women
have turned to steroids to build their
bodies.

33

Young men are expected to look a
certain way, too. Guys are supposed to
have hard, well-defined chests. They are
supposed to have washboard stomachs
and developed arms and legs. More and
more young men also turn to drugs to
help them get that look.

It is important to look good and feel
good about yourself. It is also important
to know that you can change the way
your body looks. But drugs will not do it
for you. The only way to get the body you
want is by hard work. You have to exercise and eat the right foods. A better body
can only be achieved through determination and discipline.

College Athletics

College athletes have some of the same
problems that many younger athletes
have. They feel pressure from some of
their teammates to use drugs. They want
to be accepted, too. There are some dif-
ferences, however.

Cleanliness and grooming make you look your best.

A lot of money is invested in college sports and in college athletes. Most college athletes win full or partial scholarships to play sports for their schools. Playing the sport is like having a job, because the athletes receive an education or money for college.

The coach of a team is like a boss. The athletes do what their boss tells them to do. Coaches usually want the best for their athletes. However, some coaches will do whatever it takes to win, even if winning means that some players are using steroids or other drugs.

It is wrong for a person to use drugs. | *35*
It is also wrong for a coach to pressure
an athlete to use drugs. No matter who
offers the drugs, the answer should always
be a firm no. When one player uses drugs
to compete, it starts problems for all the
players.

Some athletes do use drugs. Then
other athletes use drugs to keep things
even or "fair." But the only fair way to
play is drug-free.

Professional Sports

Professional athletes are another story. Professional sports are a big business. A lot
of money can be made or lost. Professional athletes are paid huge salaries.
Having so much money makes it possible
for them to afford drugs easily.

Pro athletes become famous. They
start to feel that they can take on the
world. Some get involved with drugs.
Then they learn that drugs can destroy
anybody, even star athletes.

CHAPTER 4

When Athletes Choose Drugs

*W*e can learn from other people's mistakes. We can learn how drugs can affect the lives of those who take them.

In 1986, Len Bias, a star basketball player at the University of Maryland, was drafted to play for the Boston Celtics. His life seemed perfect. He was young, healthy, and he had just been chosen to play for one of the best professional basketball teams in the world. He went to a party held in his honor. Someone offered Len cocaine. Len tried it. It shocked the world when he died of a heart attack soon afterward.

Steve Howe, who played for the Los Angeles Dodgers in the early 1980s, is another athlete who chose drugs. He did

Drug use may lead to dismissal from a team.

38 not die, but his life was permanently changed by drugs.

In 1980, Steve was named Rookie of the Year. He was said to be the best new professional player in Major League baseball. In 1981, Steve pitched in the World Series. The Dodgers won that year. In 1984, Steve was chosen to play in the All-Star game. He was enjoying an extremely successful career.

Then Steve became addicted to cocaine. He would drive 150 miles just to buy coke. He left his wife and children for days at a time.

In 1984, Steve was suspended from baseball because of his drug use. He entered treatment programs five times. After each treatment he went back to drugs. Steve learned that addiction is hard to fight. Once a person starts using drugs, it is very hard to stop. And the person spends the rest of his or her life fighting the urge to use them again.

Steve has stopped using drugs. That means he is a recovering drug addict. He learned the hard way how drugs can affect a person's life.

The story of Ben Johnson shows that drugs can ruin your life even when you

After winning a gold medal at the 1988 Olympics, Ben Johnson (left) tested positive for steroids. He had to give his medal to Carl Lewis (right).

think you are at your best. At the 1988 Summer Olympic Games in Seoul, South Korea, runners Ben Johnson and Carl Lewis competed in the 100-meter dash. They had raced many times before, and it was believed that this race would

40 determine which one was the fastest man in the world.

The starting gun went off and in a little less than ten seconds, the race was over. Ben Johnson took first place. He broke the world's record. He was the fastest man alive. Carl Lewis had come in second.

However, after a drug test required by the International Olympic Committee, it was discovered that Ben Johnson had cheated. He had used steroids. The gold medal was taken from Ben and given to Carl Lewis.

Ben Johnson suffered the humiliation and shame of losing the gold medal because of his drug use. He had let down the people of Canada, the country that he represented. He lost the respect of other athletes. The entire world knew that he had cheated by taking drugs.

Tony Anderson was a high school varsity football player in Valdosta, Georgia. The Valdosta Wildcats had won the state championship nineteen times. The people of Valdosta take their football seriously. They have great pride in their team. Tony was the star. They called him "Touchdown Tony." The best universities in the country offered him scholarships.

The Valdosta football team has a rule about drugs—athletes who use drugs are not allowed on the team. One day, Tony and some other players showed up drunk for a scrimmage game. The Valdosta coach stood by the rules. He kicked Tony and the other players off the team.

Tony and the others had set a bad example for the kids who looked up to the football players. Tony was a great athlete, but he was not a good role model.

Tony started to drink alcohol more often. Then he moved on to other drugs, like marijuana and cocaine. One day, he was driving a car and he hit someone. He thought the person was okay, so he drove away.

Tony was arrested for reckless driving and for leaving the scene of an accident. He was released on probation, but he had to report to a probation officer regularly. He violated his probation. Now he is in prison.

Darryl Strawberry is another Major League baseball player who was drawn to drugs and alcohol. But his story has a happy ending.

Playing for the New York Mets, Darryl started his professional career with a bang as Rookie of the Year in 1983 at the age of twenty-one. From there his career took

42 off. Before he was twenty-five, Darryl was a star and a millionaire. He was also addicted to alcohol and cocaine.

Darryl's addictions began to affect his abilities. He often was late for games and sometimes he didn't even show up. He went from the Mets to the Los Angeles Dodgers to the San Francisco Giants. He entered drug treatment centers several times. He was finally suspended from baseball for his drug use.

Darryl saw his suspension as a wake-up call. He took the time to get help, and followed a strict program of recovery. He was signed by the New York Yankees in 1996. Thanks to his decision to give up drugs and alcohol, he was able to help the Yankees do something they hadn't done since the late 1970s—win the World Series.

You've seen how using drugs and alcohol can ruin a great career. It can also ruin a person's life.

Lost Chances

Social Loss

Athletes hold a special place in the eyes of the community. They are highly respected because they have athletic talent.

Athletes are also role models. Young athletes look up to them. They want to be just as good when they get older. Non-athletes look up to them too; they admire the athlete's ability.

When athletes use drugs, they lose the respect of the people around them. They are no longer treated as heroes. Younger people no longer want to be like them.

What about the other players on the team? How do you think they treat a teammate who uses drugs? They think that he or she ruined a good thing. They have no respect for the drug user at all.

People who use drugs also lose friends. Why? Because they start acting differently. They start treating people badly. Sometimes drug users are violent. Most people don't want to be around people who change when they use drugs.

Financial Loss

Steve Howe says that he lost $5 million. He was highly paid, and he lost it all because he chose to use cocaine. Drug-using athletes can lose scholarships to college. There are high prices to be paid for drug use.

Personality Loss

Drug-using athletes lose respect and friends. They say that they feel they have

44 | lost almost everything. Drugs make most athletes lose pride in themselves. These athletes usually feel that they have let everybody down.

Most of all, drug-using athletes lose the future. They will never know how good they could have been or how far they could have gone. The world will never know if Len Bias would have been one of the greats. Ben Johnson will never know if he could have beaten Carl Lewis fairly that day at the Olympics. Tony Anderson will never know how it feels to play college football. Athletes who use drugs will always be asking, "How good could I have been if I hadn't used drugs?"

CHAPTER 5

The Best You Can Be

Who are the best athletes in the world? Everyone has a different answer. The best hockey player may be Wayne Gretzky. The best tennis player may be Monica Seles. The best football player may be Jerry Rice.

According to most people, Michael Jordan is the best basketball player. He helped his college team win an NCAA championship. He won a gold medal in the 1984 and the 1992 Olympics. He has played for the Chicago Bulls. He was Rookie of the Year in his first season. He has led his team to the national championships several times. He has set new NBA scoring records. He is a great

46 | offensive player and a great defensive player. He is the best player in the history of basketball.

One of the best gymnasts in the world is Shannon Miller. She won two gold medals for gymnastics in the 1996 Olympics, one for the balance beam and the other with the U.S. Women's Team. By the time she was 18, Shannon was the most decorated gymnast in U.S. history. She also is a top scholar who got straight As in high school.

Michael Jordan and Shannon Miller are just two of the great athletes in the world. What makes them great? They have talent. They practice long, hard hours to be the best. They also know that they can be the best without using drugs. Drugs would slow them down and would affect their health.

Top athletes stay on top by staying off drugs.

Sports, Drugs, and You

Since the beginning of time, people have been competing against each other. We compete to push each other to be better. We compete to test how far the human body can go. We want to achieve what other people can only dream of doing.

Role models should be good examples of discipline and determination for younger people.

Shannon Miller is a winner and a good role model because of
hard work and determination.

People also compete with each other because it's fun. It's great to hear the roar of a crowd at a sporting event. It's fun to work with a team to prove that you are the best. It's fun to work up a sweat battling on a tennis court.

We want to feel the thrill of victory. We also want to learn how to lose with honor. Whether we win or lose, the thrill of great competition is always there.

Playing sports gives us so much. When we are chosen for a team, we feel good about ourselves. We believe in our own talents. Even if we only play sports on the street or in school, it still feels good to be playing.

Sports also teach us discipline. To be good, you have to practice. You have to play by the rules and be healthy. You have to be willing to follow orders and work very hard. Mental and physical discipline are important to being a good athlete.

Being a good athlete also means choosing good role models. People like Michael Jordan and Shannon Miller are good role models because they don't do drugs. They work hard, and they are the best. People like Steve Howe and other drug users are bad role models. They are no longer the best at what they do. Choose

50 good role models and try to follow their road to success.

When it comes to competition, you have to rely on your natural talents, not drugs. You can also make sure that all the competitors are playing fair. You can ask that drug testing be done.

You can also report when someone on a team is using drugs. Tell your other teammates. Try to use positive peer pressure to get the user to stop. Ask the coach to talk to the team about drugs.

Nobody wants one drunk or stoned player to blow a game for the whole team. Nobody wants a teammate to be injured either. The game will be fair and fun only if every athlete is drug-free.

What Can You Do?

To be a good athlete, there are some things you need to do. The most important thing to do is to stay away from drugs.

You can ignore the people who offer the drugs. You can leave a party if people are using drugs. You can tell your friends that you care about them, and that you don't want to see them get messed up from drugs.

If you suspect that someone is using drugs, you can look for some of these warning signs:

- Family problems;
- Weight loss (cocaine, speed);
- Weight gain (steroids, alcohol);
- Shorter attention span;
- Changing circle of friends;
- Showing up late;
- Money problems;
- Depression;
- Violent or aggressive behavior;
- Lying;
- Lower performance in school and sports;
- Fatigue;
- Red eyes;
- Frequent illness.

If someone you know has a problem with drugs, you can help. You can educate yourself about drug use in many ways. Read books about drugs. Watch television shows or read news items about drug abuse. Ask your parents, teachers, and doctors about drugs. Talk to a minister or a rabbi or the local drug-abuse agency. Once you have the information, try to pass it on to the drug user. Get a list of phone numbers that can be called for help. Be prepared to answer questions about drugs with the correct information.

Just telling a drug user about the bad

52 | effects will not solve the problem. A person with a drug problem needs help. You also need to talk to the person's parents. The parents have a right to know and help.

Approaching somebody about drug use can be very difficult. You need to handle the situation with care. The person will usually deny that there is a problem. He will try to put you on the defensive by saying things like, "I thought you were my friend. Are you calling me a drug addict?" Stay calm and handle the situation.

- Do not become emotional and argue about it.
- Do not make excuses for the person.
- Do not take over his or her duties.
- Do not try to talk sense while the person is drunk or high.
- Do not accept responsibility for the person's actions.
- Do not feel guilty for his or her drug-use problem.

Find a way to feel comfortable with saying no to drugs. If you say "no" often enough, people will stop offering it. As an athlete, you have a responsibility to say no. Your team counts on you. The fans count on you. Most of all, you owe it to yourself to be the best that you can be.

Fact Sheet

- 3 million Americans have tried steroids.
- $300 to $400 million worth of steroids are sold every year.
- 60 percent of all crime is drug-related.
- Smoking is directly related to 400,000 deaths each year.
- 2 million teens aged twelve to seventeen smoke cigarettes.
- One can of beer contains as much alcohol as one ounce of liquor.
- Diet pills are drugs called amphetamines.
- One police officer fighting drugs is killed every fifty-seven hours.

54

- An estimated 30 percent of NFL players use steroids.
- Marijuana stays in the bloodstream for up to thirty days.
- The first contact with drugs is usually through a friend.
- 9 million Americans have used marijuana in the past month.
- More than 10,000 anti-drug clubs exist across the United States.
- There are eighty brands of steroids on the market today.
- One in fifteen high school seniors admitted to using steroids.
- Drinking usually starts at about age twelve.
- 25 million Americans have tried cocaine.
- Drug users make up the largest number of school dropouts.
- 50 percent of the population aged twelve and older drink alcohol.
- 1.8 million teens aged twelve to seventeen have used alcohol in the past month.
- Steroids cost between $50 and $600 per month depending on dosage.
- 93 percent of all people who have tried cocaine used marijuana first.

Glossary—
Explaining New Words

abuse Overuse of drugs in illegal or unsafe ways.

addiction Dependence on something, such as a drug or alcohol.

alcoholism Disease that causes people to become dependent on alcohol.

anabolic steroid Man-made drug that is used to increase muscle size.

central nervous system The brain, spinal cord, and nerves.

chemical dependence Disease that occurs when someone is mentally or physically dependent on a drug.

cholesterol Type of fat that can clog veins and arteries in the body.

56 | **cirrhosis** Disease of the liver that can be caused by heavy drinking.

cocaine Powerful, addictive stimulant.

crack Extremely powerful and addictive, smokable form of cocaine.

drug Any substance other than food or water which, when taken into the body, changes the way the mind or body works.

drug addict Person who is dependent on a drug other than alcohol.

experimentation Use of drugs to find out how they will affect you.

gateway drugs Drugs, such as tobacco, alcohol, and marijuana, that lead to the use of other drugs.

hormone Substance in the body that tells the body to grow or change.

injection Forcing a liquid into the body through a needle.

joint Slang word for marijuana cigarette.

marijuana Drug that is made up of the dried leaves, flowers, and stems of the hemp plant and is usually smoked.

menstrual cycle Monthly process of ovulation and menstruation in mature females.

negative peer pressure Pressure from people your age to do something that you don't want to do.

nicotine The drug in tobacco that can cause dependency.

peers People your own age.

positive peer pressure Pressure from people your age to do things that are good for you.

prescription Note that a doctor writes to a pharmacist ordering a medicine.

recover To become well.

testosterone Hormone in males that makes boys mature into men.

tolerance Becoming used to something.

Where to Go for Help

Al-Anon (for families of alcoholics)
(800) 344-2666
Web site: http://solar.rtd.utk.edu/al-anon
(this homepage is unofficial)

Alcohol Hot Line
(800) ALCOHOL [252-6465]

Cocaine Anonymous (CA)
3740 Overland Avenue
Los Angles, CA 90034
(800) 347-8998
Web site: http://www.ca.org

Cocaine Hot Line
(800) COCAINE [262-2463]

International Sports Institute and Clinic
(for treatment of steroid use)
(412) 452-9572

"Just Say NO" Hot Line
(800) 258-2766

Nar-Anon (for families of drug users)
(310) 547-5800

Narcotics Anonymous
P.O. Box 999
Van Nuys, CA 91409
(818) 997-3822
Web site: http://www.wsonic.com

National Institute on Drug Abuse (NIDA)
(800) 638-2045

National Steroid Research Center and
   Other Drugs of Abuse in Sports
(800) STEROID [783-7643]

Addictions Foundation of Manitoba
1031 Portage Avenue
Winnipeg, MB, Canada R3G 0R8
(204) 944-6200
fax: (204) 786-7768

Alcohol and Drug Dependency Information and Counseling Services (ADDICS)
#2, 24711/2 Portage Avenue
Winnipeg, MB, Canada R3J 0N6
(204) 831-1999

60 | *In Canada*

Alcohol and Drug Centre
Agassiz Branch
Chilliwack Community Services
2070 McCaffery Road
Agassiz, BC, Canada V0M 1A0
(604) 796-3431

For Further Reading

Peck, Rodney. *Crack*. Rev. ed. New York: Rosen Publishing Group, 1993.

Scott, Sharon. *How to Say No and Keep Your Friends*. Amherst, Mass.: Human Resource Development Press, 1986.

———. *When to Say Yes and Make More Friends*. Amherst, Mass.: Human Resource Development Press, 1988.

Seixas, Judith S. *Tobacco—What It Is, What It Does*. New York: Greenwillow Books, 1981.

Taylor, Barbara. *Everything You Need to Know about Alcohol*. Rev. ed. New York: Rosen Publishing Group, 1996.

62 | ## Challenging Reading

Gold, Mark. *The Facts about Drugs and Alcohol.* New York: Bantam Books, 1988.

——. *800-COCAINE.* New York: Random House, 1988.

Index

About the Author

Rodney G. Peck is a graduate of Central Michigan University. At Central Michigan he became involved with the America's PRIDE program. The program uses attractive alternatives such as dancing, singing, acting, and speaking as ways to combat drug use. Peck worked and performed with the national PRIDE team for four years. He has spoken to thousands of young people on the topics of peer pressure, self-esteem, and drug use. Currently, he is a Peace Corps Volunteer, working in drug education in Belize, Central America.

Photo Credits

Cover Photo: Stuart Rabinowitz
Photos on pages 2, 8, 14, 17, 18, 20, 28, 32, 37, 47: Dru Nadler; pages 12, 30: Chris Volpe; page 34: Jill Heisler Jacks; pages 39, 43: AP/Wide World Photos.